The Jewish Holiday ★ Treasure Trail ★

by Naomi Patz

Behrman House, Inc.

www.behrmanhouse.com

To Natasha, for her excellent ideas for the book, and to India and Sadie and Dahlia: May you always bring joy to our family and honor to the Jewish people.

—N.P.

Project Manager: Gila Gevirtz
Book and Cover Design: Terry Taylor Studio
Page Layout Print Production: Cathy Pawlowski-Ehrhardt

Copyright © 2009 by Behrman House, Inc.

Published by Behrman House, Inc.
Springfield, NJ 07081
www.behrmanhouse.com

ISBN: 978–0–87441–833–0

Manufactured in China

Library of Congress Cataloging-in-Publication Data
Patz, Naomi.
    The Jewish holiday treasure trail   /   by Naomi Patz. — 1st ed.
            p. cm.
        ISBN 978–0–87441–833–0
        1.   Fasts and feasts—Judaism—Juvenile literature.   I. Title.
    BM690.P344   2009
    296.4'3—dc22

2008038338

Contents

1 **Welcome to the Treasure Trail**
Page 4

2 **Rosh Hashanah**
Page 12

3 **Yom Kippur**
Page 24

4 **Sukkot**
Page 34

5 **Simḥat Torah**
Page 44

6 **Shabbat**
Page 52

7 **Ḥanukkah**
Page 64

8 **Tu BiShevat**
Page 76

9 **Purim**
Page 84

10 **Passover**
Page 92

11 **Yom Hashoah**
Page 104

12 **Yom Ha'atzma'ut**
Page 108

13 **Shavuot**
Page 118

✿ **Treasure Trail Stickers**
Page 129

CHAPTER 1

Welcome to the Treasure Trail

Mrs. Lubar, Daniel's religious school teacher, stood in front of the class. "Who knows about Elijah the prophet?" she asked.

"I do," said Daniel. "We have a special wine cup for him at the Passover seder."

"Excellent," said Mrs. Lubar. "The Bible tells us about Elijah and the other prophets, wise teachers who helped our people learn the lessons of the Torah. The prophets taught us to celebrate the Jewish holidays, be kind, and seek peace."

Mrs. Lubar told the class about a new Web site called ElijahRocks.net. She asked the class to visit it before each Jewish holiday.

Daniel decided to use his Virtual Plasma Interface (VPI) to go to ElijahRocks. It was invented by his Israeli cousin Rivkah's dad—Uncle Moshe. He had given Daniel the VPI when Daniel and his parents visited Rivkah and her family in Israel this past summer.

The VPI was so small that it fit into the palm of Daniel's hand. Its most awesome feature was its ability to transport people in and out of virtual worlds. That meant that Daniel could "VPI" himself to ElijahRocks.

כוס אליהו
Elijah Cup

The two Hebrew words say *kos Eliyahu*, which means "Elijah's cup." Can you point to Elijah's name on the cup?

Another great VPI feature was virtual mail (v-mail), which allowed users to send and receive messages *and* objects. Daniel and Rivkah had promised Uncle Moshe to test the VPI for a year. The project was **TOP SECRET**.

As soon as he got home from school, Daniel went to his room and VPI'd himself to ElijahRocks. The VPI screen swirled with colors, and lights flashed as Daniel was transported. When he arrived, he saw a table piled high with ancient scrolls. Sitting next to the table was a gray-haired man. He was dressed in a long robe like the ancient Jews wore and was tinkering with a round, computer-like object that was half the size of a baseball. "That must be Elijah," Daniel thought. "Wow, Elijah rocks!"

The man looked up and said, "Shalom, Daniel. I'm Elijah. Sorry, but I'm a little busy now. Why don't you invite Rivkah

to join you, and select the Treasure Trail. We can talk another time, after you've both been to the trail.

Daniel was stunned. Elijah knew his name and his cousin Rivkah. Daniel was learning that weird things happen when you use a VPI. He v-mailed Rivkah and she agreed to join him.

When Rivkah arrived, she and Daniel used their VPIs to select the Treasure Trail. They landed on a HUGE game board, which had the names of all the Jewish holidays on it. The cousins looked at each other in wonder. But before they could say anything, instructions appeared.

Dear Daniel and Rivkah,
Welcome to the Treasure Trail!

There are twelve stops on the trail—one for each Jewish holiday. At each stop, a riddle will appear. Along the way you will receive help in solving the riddles. Good luck!

Elijah

"Sounds great," said Rivkah. "I can't wait to try it out for Rosh Hashanah. But now I really need to go and study. I've got a math test tomorrow." The cousins waved goodbye and VPI'd themselves home. Elijah smiled, knowing that they would return soon.

Start

10

The Jewish year is divided into twelve months: Tishre, Ḥeshvan, Kislev, Tevet, Shevat, Adar, Nisan, Iyar, Sivan, Tammuz, Av, and Elul. An extra month, called Second Adar, is added on leap years. Second Adar comes right after Adar (which, in leap years, is called First Adar).

Tishre תִּשְׁרֵי

Sukkot

Simḥat Torah

Purim

Ḥeshvan חֶשְׁוָן

Shabbat

Shabbat

Adar אֲדָר

Kislev כִּסְלֵו

Shevat שְׁבָט

Leap Year! Second Adar

Ḥanukkah

Tevet טֵבֵת

Tu BiShevat

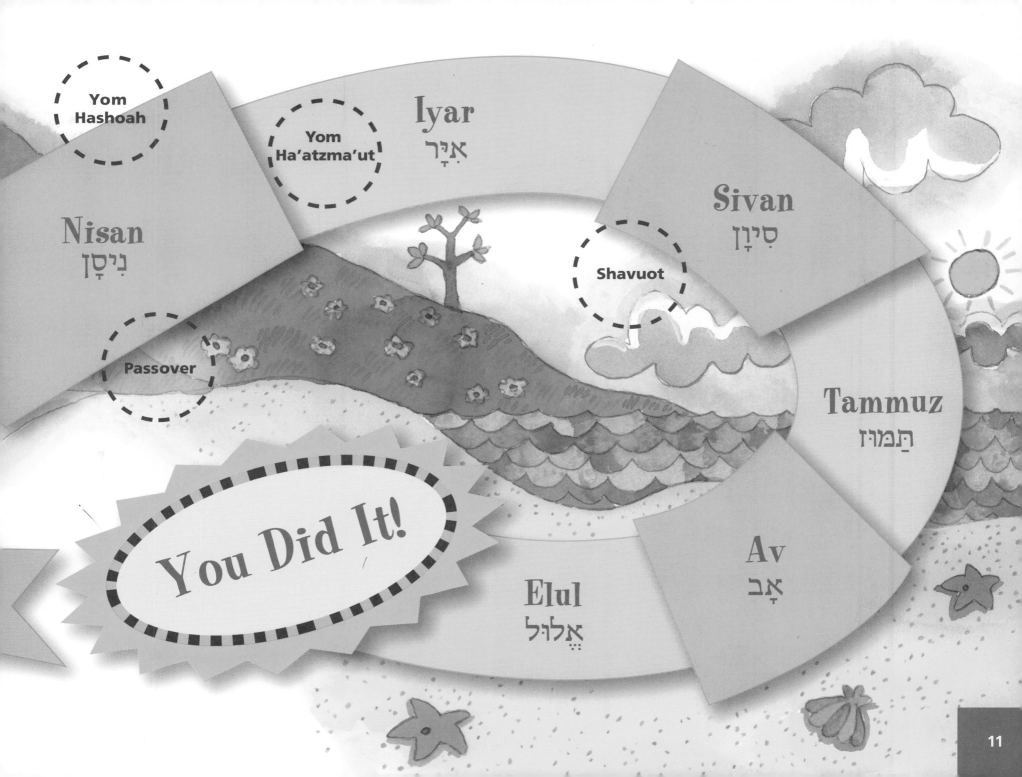

Tishre	**1**	תִּשְׁרֵי
Ḥeshvan		חֶשְׁוָן
Kislev		כִּסְלֵו
Tevet		טֵבֵת
Shevat		שְׁבָט
Adar		אֲדָר
Nisan		נִיסָן
Iyar		אִיָּר
Sivan		סִיוָן
Tammuz		תַּמּוּז
Av		אָב
Elul		אֱלוּל

CHAPTER 2

רֹאשׁ הַשָּׁנָה

Rosh Hashanah

The day before Rosh Hashanah, Daniel v-mailed Rivkah. She didn't answer, so he went to ElijahRocks by himself. Elijah greeted him, "Shalom. You're just in time. The first holiday of the Jewish year is almost here."

"Yes," Daniel answered, "Rosh Hashanah, the New Year."

Heading Out for a Good Year

Rosh (רֹאשׁ) means "head" or "beginning," and *shanah* (שָׁנָה) means "year." On Rosh Hashanah, we celebrate the beginning of the Jewish year. Like the start of the school year, Rosh Hashanah comes at the end of summer or beginning of autumn. We send greeting cards to wish our friends a **shanah tovah** (שָׁנָה טוֹבָה), a "good year."

Put a good thought in your *rosh* by describing one thing you can do to help make the New Year a good year for a friend.

_____

_____

_____

_____

"Great. Can you tell me the other names of the holiday?" asked Elijah. Seeing Daniel's confusion, Elijah asked, "How many names do *you* have?"

"Lots," Daniel answered proudly. "My first name is Daniel. My middle name is Jonathan. My Hebrew name is Dani'el Yonatan. My family name is Friedman. My teachers call me Danny, and my friends call me Dan the Hoopin' Man."

"Well," Elijah said, "Rosh Hashanah has *three* other names. Tell me what you know about Rosh Hashanah. Then I'll tell you the other names."

Happy Birthday, World!

Rosh Hashanah begins on the first day of the Hebrew month of Tishre. It is the birthday of the world. We thank God for all of Creation, including nature's beauty, and for our family, teachers, and friends.

Name two people or things you want to thank God for on Rosh Hashanah. Explain why.

1. _____

   _____

2. _____

   _____

"On Rosh Hashanah, we remember the good we have done in the past year," Daniel began. "We also remember our mistakes and apologize to anyone we have hurt. We think about how to avoid making the same mistakes in the new year. Finally, we forgive those who apologize for having hurt us."

"Exactly!" Elijah exclaimed. "Reminding ourselves of what we have done can help us do better, so one name for Rosh Hashanah is the Day of Remembering, **Yom Hazikaron**."

The prophet continued, "Jewish tradition teaches us to imagine that God records our behavior in a giant book, called the **Book of Life.** On Rosh Hashanah, we are told, God reviews the book—our behavior, apologies, and efforts to improve. Judaism teaches that

Noah is five. He asked for a birthday cake shaped like a soccer ball because he loves soccer. If the world celebrated its birthday with a cake, what might the cake look like? Why? What birthday wish do you think the world would make? Why?

we are responsible for what we do but can be forgiven for our mistakes. So the holiday is also called the Day of Judgment, **Yom Hadin**."

"There's something else," Daniel said. "On Rosh Hashanah we go to synagogue prayer services and listen to the blowing of the **shofar** (שׁוֹפָר)."

"Excellent," Elijah said. "Three different calls are sounded by the shofar. They are **teki'ah** (one long blast), **shevarim** (three medium blasts), and **teru'ah** (nine short blasts). The final blast in a series of calls is the great teki'ah, **teki'ah gedolah.**

"In many synagogues, 100 blasts of the shofar are heard during the morning prayer service. So another name for Rosh Hashanah is the Day of the Sounding of the Shofar, **Yom Teru'ah**."

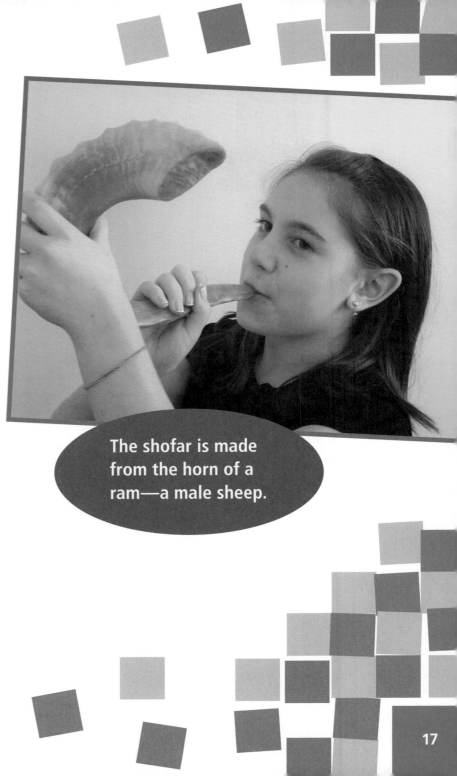

The shofar is made from the horn of a ram—a male sheep.

"One more thing," Daniel said. "After services, we go to a nearby stream, lake, or ocean. We throw bread crumbs into the water as if we were getting rid of our mistakes. This custom is called **tashlich,** which means 'throwing' or 'sending away.' Throwing bread crumbs into the water doesn't make us better people. But it can remind us that if we make an effort, we can get rid of bad habits and make a fresh start on Rosh Hashanah."

Rosh Hashanah begins in the evening. Before we eat, we recite the blessings over the holiday candles, wine, and ḥallah. We also say the Sheheḥeyanu. This blessing thanks God for life and for allowing us to reach this joyous time.

On Rosh Hashanah, we dip apples in honey for a sweet year. We also eat a large, round ḥallah, a reminder of the circle of the year. The ḥallah looks like a crown, reminding us that God is the Ruler of the world.

The Name Game

Many people send New Year's cards to family and friends, wishing them a shanah tovah.

Draw a line from each holiday name to its matching card.

Rosh Hashanah   Yom Hadin   Yom Teru'ah   Yom Hazikaron

This handmade Israeli New Year's card is written in script letters. It says, "Shanah Tovah."

Rosh Hashanah Riddle

In the season known as fall, how do we answer the shofar's call?

"Here's Rivkah," Elijah announced. And with that, the prophet vanished. The cousins immediately selected the Treasure Trail and landed on the huge game board. A riddle appeared.

When the riddle faded, the cousins found themselves transported to a synagogue. The people inside were praying from the Rosh Hashanah prayer book, the **maḥazor** (מַחְזוֹר). A boy stood beside them, just outside the doorway. He looked very sad.

Seeing Daniel and Rivkah, the boy shyly said, "Can you help me? I am sorry about the mean things I did this year. I know the Hebrew alphabet but I can't read the prayers. How can I apologize to God?"

"Don't worry," Rivkah said. "You can talk to God by praying in your own way."

The boy's eyes lit up. He quickly went into the synagogue and in a strong voice began to recite the letters of the Hebrew alphabet. People grumbled, "Be quiet!" "Sit down!"

"Let the boy be," said the rabbi. "Each letter he recites is a prayer from the heart. The shofar calls each of us to take responsibility for our actions, ask for forgiveness, and try to become a better person. Because of *his* prayers, *our* sins may be forgiven, too."
(This story is based on a Ḥasidic tale.)

"That's the answer to the riddle," said Rivkah. "We answer the shofar's call by admitting that we have made mistakes, apologizing, and trying to do better!"

"Yes!" said Daniel, who, a moment later, was stunned to find himself in his bedroom. It seemed that solving the riddle had transported him home. He had not even had to use his VPI. But where was Rivkah? Daniel dashed off a v-mail to her.

"I'm home, too," Rivkah v-mailed back, along with a jar of honey. "Have a shanah tovah!"

"And a sweet year to you," Daniel replied.

 There is a sticker page at the end of this book. When your teacher says it is OK, turn to the Treasure Trail on pages 10–11 and place the Rosh Hashanah sticker in the correct spot.

 **www.ElijahRocks.net**

	Tishre	10	תִּשְׁרֵי
Ḥeshvan			חֶשְׁוָן
Kislev			כִּסְלֵו
Tevet			טֵבֵת
Shevat			שְׁבָט
Adar			אֲדָר
Nisan			נִיסָן
Iyar			אִיָּר
Sivan			סִיוָן
Tammuz			תַּמּוּז
Av			אָב
Elul			אֱלוּל

CHAPTER 3

Yom Kippur

A few days after Rosh Hashanah, Rivkah went to ElijahRocks. "Shalom," Elijah welcomed her. "I hope you had a nice holiday. Do you know that Rosh Hashanah and Yom Kippur are called the **High Holy Days,** or High Holidays?"

"Yes," answered Rivkah, "and Yom Kippur is the holiest day of the year."

"That's right. Also, the ten days from Rosh Hashanah through Yom Kippur are called the Ten Days of Repentance,

Sometimes, it may feel hard to say we are sorry. But after apologizing, we usually feel a lot better. Why might it be hard to apologize at first? Why might we feel better afterward?

Aseret Yemay Teshuvah," explained Elijah. "To repent is to say that you are sorry. The Hebrew word for repentance is **teshuvah** (תְּשׁוּבָה). When we make, or do, teshuvah we return to God's kind and loving ways. Teshuvah opens the door for us to become our best selves.

There are three steps to teshuvah:

1. Apologize for our mistakes.
2. Try to make up for what we did wrong.
3. Find ways to do better in the future.

"In order to do, or make, teshuvah to God, we must first make teshuvah to the people whom we have hurt. We help others make teshuvah by accepting their apologies.

"Yom Kippur begins in the evening, at home," said Elijah. "But in one way it is unlike most other holidays: On Yom Kippur, we eat *before* we light the holiday candles. Here's why:

Nighttime Is the Right Time to Begin

The word for evening or eve in Hebrew is *erev.* Jewish holidays begin in the evening. So, for example, when Yom Kippur day is on a Monday, erev Yom Kippur is on the night before, Sunday evening.

In Hebrew, the beginning of Yom Kippur is called erev Yom Kippur and the beginning of Shabbat is erev Shabbat. Name the beginning of Rosh Hashanah:

_____   _____   _____

Circle the time of day when Jewish holidays begin:

"Yom Kippur is a **fast day,** a day when adults do not eat. So we eat dinner before the holiday begins. After we light the candles, we do not eat or drink. Instead, we use our time to pray and think about how we can improve ourselves. Young children and other people for whom it would not be healthy to fast do not fast. But they may choose to eat a bit less than usual or not eat their favorite foods on Yom Kippur.

27

It is a tradition to light yahrzeit candles on certain Jewish holidays and on the anniversary of a family member's death. On the holidays, why might we particularly want to remember loved ones who have died?

"Before going to synagogue, we light the holiday candles. Some people also light a **yahrzeit candle,** a thick white candle in a container. It helps us remember the people we love who have died. A yahrzeit candle burns for at least twenty-four hours.

"We spend most of Yom Kippur in the synagogue. To show that we want a fresh start, some rabbis and cantors wear white robes. Many other worshippers also wear white clothing.

"Yom Kippur means 'Day of Atonement.' Reciting the Yom Kippur prayers helps us to come closer to God and to be 'at one' with God and God's kind and loving ways. Every year on the High Holy Days, we promise to do better in the new year.

Yizkor

On Yom Kippur, at a synagogue prayer service called **Yizkor** (יִזְכּוֹר), we respectfully and lovingly remember people who have died.

"But no one is perfect. On erev Yom Kippur, in the synagogue, we recite the **Kol Nidre** prayer. *Kol nidre* means 'all our promises.' The prayer asks God to forgive us for the promises that we are not able to keep.

"In many synagogues, all the Torah scrolls are taken out of the Holy Ark, the **Aron Hakodesh,** for Kol Nidre. They are held next to the cantor or other person who chants the prayer's beautiful melody.

"Another Yom Kippur prayer is the **Al Ḥet.** Ḥet means 'sin' or 'missing the mark'—like an arrow that misses the bull's-eye on a target. When we recite the Al Ḥet, we admit that sometimes our actions miss the target of good behavior. Sometimes we are selfish instead of generous, rude instead of polite, and mean instead of kind.

"When we recite the Al Ḥet, we say to God that we are sorry not only for the wrongs we have done but also for the mistakes that others have made. We share responsibility for each other's misdeeds.

Torah scrolls are usually dressed in colorful wraps, called mantles. On the High Holy Days, they are dressed in *white* mantles to remind us that the Torah teaches us how to live good lives.

It is *impossible* to always hit a bull's-eye but hard work makes it *possible* to become a better person. Why does it feel good to be you? What can you do to feel even better about yourself?

29

"**Avinu Malkaynu** is a prayer that is sung several times during the High Holy Days. It asks God to forgive us for our mistakes the way a loving parent does.

Tzedakah

On Yom Kippur, we think about how we can become better people. One important way is to be generous to those in need. This sharing is called **tzedakah** (צְדָקָה).

When we donate food, clothing, or toys to people who are homeless, we are giving tzedakah. And when we contribute our time and our talent by visiting or entertaining elderly or sick people, we are giving tzedakah.

Inside the helping hand, draw or write one way you can give tzedakah.

"We read the Book of Jonah from the Bible. It teaches that God wants to forgive us so that we can improve our behavior. When we forgive people who apologize to us, we give them a chance to do teshuvah and to improve their behavior.

"Jewish tradition asks us to pray and to study the Torah's lessons of goodness and kindness on Yom Kippur from early morning until dark. In many synagogues, prayer services last until three stars can be seen in the night sky. At the end of the service, one long blast of the shofar—the teki'ah gedolah—is blown. It wishes us a good New Year and reminds us of all that we have prayed for and promised.

"Then we get together with our family and friends to end the fast by sharing a **break fast** meal. Together we eat foods

The Shofar's Call

Inside the shofar, write one way in which you would like to be kinder or more helpful to a family member or friend in the new year.

such as bagels, cream cheese, lox, and salad, and we look forward to a new beginning.

"Rivkah, Daniel just arrived," said Elijah. "He looks ready to go to the trail." The cousins quickly selected the Treasure Trail, landed on the board, and . . .

Yom Kippur Riddle

On Yom Kippur, what word is key? What says, "I'll come back to you if you return to Me"?

When the riddle faded, the cousins were in the countryside. They saw a beautiful but sad-looking princess. She told them that she had argued with her parents and had run away from home. Now, she was tired and lonely and did not think her parents would forgive her.

Suddenly a messenger arrived on a great white horse. He said, "The king and queen have declared that if you return as far as you can, they will come the rest of the way to meet you." *(This story is based on a midrash from* Pesikta Rabbati.*)*

"Return! Teshuvah! That's the answer to the riddle," Daniel said. "God is like a loving parent who will come to us if we take as many steps of teshuvah as we can."

And, just as before, by solving the riddle Rivkah and Daniel were each transported home. Before going to synagogue, Rivkah did teshuvah by v-mailing Daniel an apology for having sent his birthday greeting a day late. "No problem," Daniel wrote back. "You're still my cousin *and* my best friend."

 When your teacher says it is OK, turn to the Treasure Trail on pages 10–11 and place the Yom Kippur sticker in the correct spot.

 www.ElijahRocks.net

33

Tishre	**15**	תִּשְׁרֵי
Ḥeshvan		חֶשְׁוָן
Kislev		כִּסְלֵו
Tevet		טֵבֵת
Shevat		שְׁבָט
Adar		אֲדָר
Nisan		נִיסָן
Iyar		אִיָּר
Sivan		סִיוָן
Tammuz		תַּמוּז
Av		אָב
Elul		אֱלוּל

CHAPTER 4

סֻכּוֹת

Sukkot

With only four days from the end of Yom Kippur to erev Sukkot, there wasn't much time to prepare for the festival. Daniel helped his parents set up their **sukkah** (סֻכָּה), the traditional outdoor hut that Jews build for Sukkot. Daniel and his parents decorated it with colorful autumn fruits and vegetables, like apples, grapes, peppers, and squash.

Then they picked up the **lulav** and **etrog** that they had ordered from their synagogue. Daniel knew that a lulav is made from branches of three kinds of trees: palm, myrtle, and willow. The etrog looks like a large, bumpy lemon.

A Picture-Perfect Sukkah

Sukkot lasts for a week. On Sukkot, we eat as many meals as possible in a sukkah. Some people even sleep in their sukkah! We also perform the mitzvah of inviting guests—*hachnasat orḥim*—by asking friends and family to eat in our sukkah.

Every sukkah has at least three walls. The roof is made of branches so that we can see the sky. A sukkah can be built in a backyard, on a balcony, or on the roof of a building. We decorate a sukkah with fruits and vegetables, strings of popcorn, and pictures.

Many families use an etrog that was grown in Israel and shipped to North America for Sukkot.

On the morning before Sukkot, Rivkah v-mailed Daniel from ElijahRocks. "I'm helping Elijah decorate his sukkah," she said. "Please bring a bunch of purple grapes with you." When Daniel told her that he couldn't be there until the afternoon, she wrote back, "No problem. Just v-mail the grapes to me."

When Daniel arrived at ElijahRocks, he was pleased to see the grapes hanging in the sukkah. (Although it seemed that Rivkah had eaten a few before hanging the bunch.)

Rivkah was talking with Elijah. "I know two reasons why we build a sukkah," she said. "First, God freed our ancestors from slavery in Egypt about 3,000 years ago. For the next forty years, our ancestors wandered in the desert and slept in huts called *sukkot*.

"Second, most of our ancestors were farmers in the Land of Israel. In the autumn they harvested their grape, date, and olive crops. They had no time to go home because they had to finish their work before the rains came. So they built huts in their fields and slept in them."

Jews around the world celebrate Sukkot. This picture shows a meal being served in the Grand Choral Synagogue sukkah in Saint Petersburg, Russia.

You're the Artist!

Decorate the sukkah below. Inside it, write the names of two guests you would like to invite for the holiday. Why did you choose those people?

Olives are still grown in Israel and they are sold around the world. When planning your holiday menu you may want to buy olives and olive oil that were produced in Israel.

"The holiday is named for those huts," Daniel added. "It is also called **Zeman Simḥataynu,** Time of Our Happiness, and **Ḥag Ha'asif**, Harvest Festival. The harvest reminds us of all we have to be happy about."

"Good job, kids," said Elijah. "In ancient times, Jews from all over Israel went up to the Temple in Jerusalem to thank God for the harvest. They brought a goat or sheep or some flour or wine as an offering of thanks to God. Musicians played flutes, harps, and drums, and people danced and sang praises to God."

An American-Style Sukkot

The early American settlers who created the holiday of Thanksgiving knew the Bible. They used Sukkot as the model for a holiday to thank God for their harvest. What tradition might you add to your Thanksgiving celebration to remind you that the holiday is modeled after Sukkot?

_____

_____

A Festival on Foot

A pilgrim is someone who walks or travels to a holy place. The trip is called a "pilgrimage." Sukkot is one of the three pilgrimage festivals in the Jewish calendar. (The other two are in the spring—Passover and Shavuot.) *Regel* is the Hebrew word for "foot," so in Hebrew the three pilgrimage festivals are called the Shalosh Regalim. *Shalosh* means "three," and *regalim* means "feet."

Name the three pilgrimage holidays by writing one name in each footprint below.

On erev Sukkot, before we eat, we recite the blessings over the candles, wine, and hallah. Whether we eat in a sukkah or in our home, we can recite these blessings. But if we sit in a sukkah, we recite an additional blessing for that mitzvah.

"But why do *we* celebrate Sukkot? We aren't farmers," said Daniel.

"True," Elijah said. "But like our ancestors, we have a lot to be grateful for: good food—fruits, cereal, and cheese; warm clothes—sweaters, gloves, and scarves; and people who care about us—family, friends, and teachers. And like our ancestors, we thank God for all the good in our lives.

Today, instead of using our feet to carry us on a pilgrimage to the Temple in Jerusalem, we can celebrate Sukkot by using our feet to carry us to synagogue services and bring food to the needy.

The Prayer Service

On Sukkot, many Jews bring an etrog and lulav to synagogue and recite the blessing over them. We also read from the Torah to learn how our ancestors celebrated the holiday and how we can celebrate it. We recite prayers of thanks, called **Hallel** (הַלֵּל). The word *halleluyah* is a Hebrew word that means "praise God."

Shemini Atzeret

At the end of Sukkot we celebrate **Shemini Atzeret.** On this day, we pray for rain to prepare the ground for planting. In some congregations, Shemini Atzeret is a separate day. In others, the Shemini Atzeret prayers are part of the celebration of Simḥat Torah, which is the next holiday you will learn about.

"Another way we show our thanks is by giving Tzedakah to those who are less fortunate. We can contribute canned food to a food bank or donate toys and books to a hospital.

"Like so many Jewish holidays, Sukkot is filled with both joy and giving," said Elijah. "*Ḥag* is the Hebrew word for 'holiday' or 'festival.' *Samayaḥ* means 'happy.' On Jewish holidays we wish one another a **ḥag samayaḥ,** a happy holiday. So, here goes—ḥag samayaḥ." With that Elijah disappeared, and Daniel and Rivkah selected the Treasure Trail.

Sukkot Riddle

What makes the world more right and fair? What teaches us that we must share?

When the words faded, Rivkah and Daniel were standing at the edge of a wheat field in ancient Jerusalem. They saw two men carrying stalks of wheat in opposite directions across the field. In the dark, neither man saw the other because they were moving along different paths.

A wise owl in a nearby tree explained, "The two men are brothers who work this field. The younger brother is not married. He is concerned that his older, married brother will not have enough food with which to feed his wife and six children. So he is putting a portion of his harvest on his brother's pile.

"But the older brother is concerned about his unmarried brother. He worries that there may be no one to care for his brother when he is old. So he is putting a portion of *his* harvest on his brother's pile so that his brother will have more for the future."

The owl's soft hoot caught the brothers' attention. As they moved toward the owl's tree, they saw each other. Each immediately understood what the other had been doing. They lay down their wheat and hugged. *(This story is based on a Jewish legend.)*

"I've got it!" said Rivkah. "It is right and fair to share our harvest with people who are in need. The answer to the riddle is Tzedakah."

Daniel reached out to give Rivkah a high five but—oops!—he was standing in his family's sukkah. He was home and ready to celebrate Sukkot!

➡ *When your teacher says it is OK, turn to the Treasure Trail on pages 10–11 and place the Sukkot sticker in the correct spot.*

www.ElijahRocks.net

Tishre 22/23 — תִּשְׁרֵי

Ḥeshvan	חֶשְׁוָן
Kislev	כִּסְלֵו
Tevet	טֵבֵת
Shevat	שְׁבָט
Adar	אֲדָר
Nisan	נִיסָן
Iyar	אִיָּר
Sivan	סִיוָן
Tammuz	תַּמּוּז
Av	אָב
Elul	אֱלוּל

CHAPTER 5

שִׂמְחַת תּוֹרָה

Simḥat Torah

Mrs. Lubar introduced the guest who stood in front of Daniel's religious school class. "Mr. Cohen is a scribe, a **sofer.** A sofer writes the letters of the **Torah** (תּוֹרָה) by hand on Torah scrolls. He uses a quill pen made from a sharpened turkey feather, which he dips in black ink. A sofer works slowly to avoid making mistakes."

Mr. Cohen demonstrated how to write a Torah scroll. Daniel helped by writing the Hebrew letter alef with a quill pen. After class, Daniel went to ElijahRocks. He told Elijah about the sofer's visit.

Picture twenty-five six-foot-tall people lying head to toe. That's how long some Torah scrolls are when they are unrolled.

Name two people whose stories are written in every Torah scroll.

_____

This photograph shows a sofer and his helper working on a Torah scroll. Torah scrolls are written on many pieces of parchment—usually made of sheepskin—which are sewn together.

"Sounds great," said Elijah. "The Torah teaches us the **mitzvot** (מִצְוֹת), God's instructions on how to live as Jews and become the best people we can be. The Torah also tells wonderful stories about our ancestors."

"I know a lot of stories from the Torah," Daniel said proudly. "I know the story of the Creation of the world, and Noah and the flood. I know about Abraham and Sarah, their son Isaac and his wife Rebecca, and their grandson Jacob and his wives Rachel and Leah. . . ."

What's Your Favorite?

Inside the scroll, draw a picture of your favorite story from the Torah.

These fruits are pomegranates. Our tradition teaches that pomegranates have as many seeds as there are mitzvot in the Torah—613! Some Torah scrolls are dressed with silver decorations called *rimonim,* meaning "pomegranates." (See the photograph to the right.)

The rimonim remind us of the Torah's mitzvot.

"Very good," said Elijah. He then explained that the Torah is the first five books of the Bible. "Each book is divided into portions. We read one portion in synagogue every Shabbat. It takes a year to read the entire Torah. Then we start again!" said Elijah. "Simḥat Torah is the day we finish the last portion and begin again by reading the first words of the Torah. Simḥat Torah means 'Joy of the Torah.'"

Among the mitzvot that the Torah teaches is kindness to animals, tza'ar ba'alei ḥayim. This public water dish is in Tel Aviv, Israel. It is there for dogs that are thirsty.

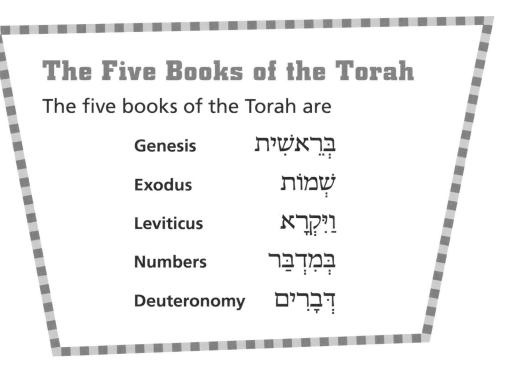

The Five Books of the Torah

The five books of the Torah are

Genesis	בְּרֵאשִׁית
Exodus	שְׁמוֹת
Leviticus	וַיִּקְרָא
Numbers	בְּמִדְבַּר
Deuteronomy	דְּבָרִים

Rivkah arrived and joined the conversation. "We take all the Torah scrolls out of the synagogue's Ark on Simḥat Torah," she said. "People march seven times around the sanctuary carrying the Torah scrolls. The parades are called **hakafot**."

On Simḥat Torah many synagogues welcome new students to the mitzvah of Jewish learning, **Talmud Torah,** by holding a Consecration ceremony.

Welcome to Talmud Torah!

Describe two things you now know about the Jewish holidays that you didn't know when you began religious school.

1._____

2._____

"That's what we do, too," piped in Daniel. "We sing and dance as we parade with the Torah scrolls around the sanctuary." Then Daniel noticed that Elijah had disappeared. So he and Rivkah selected the Treasure Trail.

Simhat Torah Riddle

What teaches us the Jewish way? What gift from God guides us each day?

When the riddle faded, Rivkah and Daniel were surprised to find themselves crouched behind a rock, peeking at two men dressed in clothes from ancient times. One seemed angry. He yelled, "What do you mean you can't? Everyone says that you, Hillel, are the wisest teacher. If so, teach me the whole Torah while I stand on one foot and I'll become a Jew."

"OK," answered Hillel. "Do not do to other people what you don't want them to do to you. That is the whole Torah. All the rest is explanation. Now, go and study it." *(This story comes from the Talmud,* Shabbat 31a.*)*

"Torah! That's the answer to Elijah's riddle," said Rivkah.

"Yup," Daniel said as he was transported back to his religious school.

When your teacher says it is OK, turn to the Treasure Trail on pages 10–11 and place the Simḥat Torah sticker in the correct spot.

www.ElijahRocks.net

Sunday	יוֹם רִאשׁוֹן
Monday	יוֹם שֵׁנִי
Tuesday	יוֹם שְׁלִישִׁי
Wednesday	יוֹם רְבִיעִי
Thursday	יוֹם חֲמִישִׁי
Friday	יוֹם שִׁשִׁי
Shabbat	שַׁבָּת

CHAPTER 6

שַׁבָּת

Shabbat

For weeks, Daniel and Rivkah were so busy with school, sports, music lessons, and homework that they didn't go to ElijahRocks. Finally, on Thanksgiving, after the big meal, Daniel v-mailed his cousin, "Tomorrow is erev Shabbat. Let's visit Elijah. I bet there's a Shabbat stop on the Treasure Trail."

As soon as they logged on, Elijah appeared. "I was just planning Shabbat dinner for my guests who are coming tomorrow," he said.

Before lighting the Shabbat candles many Jews put money in a Tzedakah box. Why is sharing with people who are in need a way to thank God for all the good in our lives?

"It's awesome that every week we have a holiday," Daniel said. "The Ten Commandments tell us to observe Shabbat. Imagine, on Shabbat it's a mitzvah to eat yummy foods, be happy, and relax!"

Rivkah continued, "The Book of Genesis says that 'in six days, God created the heavens and the earth and everything in them.' Then, on the seventh day, God rested. So Shabbat became a day of rest for people—and for animals, too.

"We begin Shabbat by lighting at least two candles and saying the blessing over them," Rivkah went on. "After that my mother recites the blessing over me. She asks God to watch over me and bless my life with peace."

"Then it's time for the blessing over wine," Daniel jumped in. "It's called **Kiddush** (קִדּוּשׁ), which means 'make holy.' God blessed the seventh day and made it a holy day of rest."

"Wine is a symbol of joy," Elijah told them. "When our people were slaves in Egypt, they could not celebrate Shabbat. They didn't get *any* days off. When we say the Kiddush, we remember that a long time ago we were slaves. We thank God that we are now free."

"After Kiddush, it's almost time to eat!" said Daniel. "But first we say the blessing over the ḥallah (חַלָּה)—the **Motzi.** Then we eat our favorite Shabbat meal: soup, roast chicken, and noodle pudding. After dessert, we sing Shabbat songs. Then we recite **Birkat Hamazon,** the Grace After Meals, to thank God for our lives, our food, and Jerusalem."

We can recite Kiddush over wine or grape juice.

"My family goes to synagogue prayer services on Friday night," said Rivkah. "I love to sing **Lecha Dodi.** It says that Shabbat is like a bride who visits us. I also like the fruit and brownies at the **oneg Shabbat,** the snack after services," she added.

"*My* family goes to synagogue on Saturday morning," said Daniel. "At services, we recite Shabbat prayers. We also take the Torah out of the Ark and read the weekly portion. Some weeks there is a special celebration, like a baby naming or a bat or bar mitzvah. After services, there is *always* a snack or light meal, called a kiddush, which includes wine and ḥallah. Like an oneg Shabbat, the kiddush has tasty foods and time to hang out with friends."

We cover the ḥallah with a beautiful cloth and then uncover it before reciting the Motzi.

Shabbat Shalom

On Shabbat we greet each other by saying, **"Shabbat shalom"** (שַׁבָּת שָׁלוֹם), meaning "May you have a peaceful Shabbat." Enjoying a peaceful time—especially with our family—is a wonderful way to spend Shabbat afternoon. We can walk, read, or play board games together. When we add peace to our home by being kind and respectful to our family, we perform the mitzvah of **sh'lom bayit.**

In synagogue, it is an honor to be called up to recite the blessing over the Torah, to read from the Torah, or to dress the Torah scroll or return it to the Ark. What does this tell you about how the Jewish people feel about the Torah?

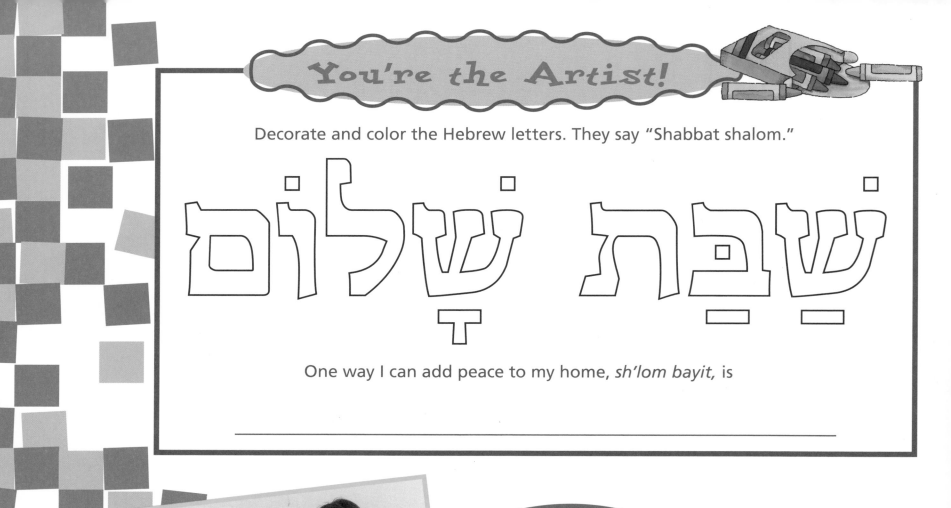

You're the Artist!

Decorate and color the Hebrew letters. They say "Shabbat shalom."

שַׁבָּת שָׁלוֹם

One way I can add peace to my home, *sh'lom bayit,* is

_____

Reciting havdalah is how we say goodbye to Shabbat until the next week. Many Jews wait until they see three stars in the sky before saying the havdalah blessings.

"Now tell me how Shabbat ends," Elijah said.

Rivkah answered. "We make **havdalah** (הַבְדָּלָה) on Saturday night. It separates the end of Shabbat from the beginning of the new week. We light the braided candle, which has at least two wicks. We smell the spice box, which is filled with cinnamon and cloves. Then we take a sip from a cup of wine. Just as we begin Shabbat with wine, so we also end it with wine."

"What I like doing most after havdalah," said Rivkah with a wink to Elijah, "is singing the song 'Elijah the Prophet,' *Eliyahu Hanavi.* We pray that one day Elijah will help bring peace to the world so that every day will be like Shabbat."

A Good Wish for the Week

After havdalah, we say, *"shavua tov,"* which means, "May you have a good week!" Describe one thing that makes a week good for you. Then tell why.

_____

_____

_____

_____

It's a Match

Draw a line from each picture to the word or words that describe it.

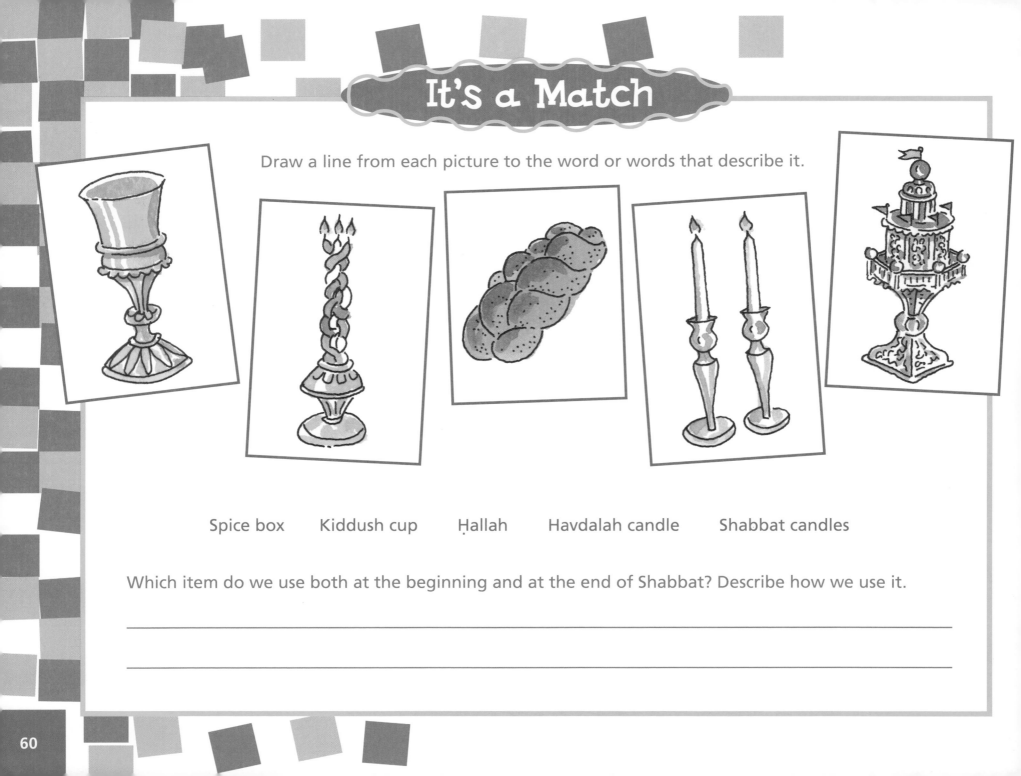

Spice box   Kiddush cup   Ḥallah   Havdalah candle   Shabbat candles

Which item do we use both at the beginning and at the end of Shabbat? Describe how we use it.

_____

_____

Elijah smiled and wished the cousins a Shabbat shalom. Then he vanished. Daniel and Rivkah wasted no time. They immediately selected the Treasure Trail.

Shabbat Riddle

When you honor the seventh day, what is sure to come your way?

When the riddle faded, Rivkah and Daniel were standing in a huge, old-fashioned kitchen. They were surprised to see that they were each wearing a chef's hat and a long apron. Then several cooks dressed like them entered the room.

The head chef was saying, "As you know, the king L-O-V-E-S to eat. Well, last Saturday, he had lunch at a rabbi's home. The meal was so good that the king ordered the rabbi to give him the recipes. Now we must prepare the meal."

Rivkah and Daniel joined in the cooking. When they finished and had placed their last platter on the table, they ducked behind a curtain and peeked out. As the king tasted one dish after another, they watched his face go from healthy pink to FIERCE white to A N G R Y red.

"This does not taste like the rabbi's food," shouted the king. The chef assured the king that he had carefully followed the recipes, so the king summoned the rabbi.

When the rabbi arrived, the king yelled, "What was in your food that is not in the recipes?"

"Shabbat spice," the rabbi answered respectfully.

"Where can I buy it?" bellowed the king.

The rabbi shook his head and said, "You cannot buy it. Shabbat spice is a gift to all who celebrate Shabbat. It's like a pinch of extra flavor that adds peace and delight to the day."

(This story is based on Midrash Rabbah, Genesis 11:4 and from the Talmud, Shabbat 119a.)

Rivkah whispered to Daniel, "The peace and delight of Shabbat are the answers to the riddle!" Daniel smiled and was transported home in a flash, ready to greet Shabbat.

 When your teacher says it is OK, turn to the Treasure Trail on pages 10–11 and place the Shabbat sticker in the correct spot.

www.ElijahRocks.net

Tishre	תִּשְׁרֵי
Ḥeshvan	חֶשְׁוָן
Kislev 25	כִּסְלֵו
Tevet	טֵבֵת
Shevat	שְׁבָט
Adar	אֲדָר
Nisan	נִיסָן
Iyar	אִיָּר
Sivan	סִיוָן
Tammuz	תַּמּוּז
Av	אָב
Elul	אֶלוּל

CHAPTER 7

חֲנֻכָּה

Ḥanukkah

It was the night before Ḥanukkah. Daniel looked forward to playing **dreidel** and eating potato pancakes, **latkes,** for eight days. Tonight Daniel was polishing the Ḥanukkah menorah, the ḥanukkiyah (חֲנֻכִּיָּה).

In the storage box for the ḥanukkiyah, Daniel found two dreidels. Both had four Hebrew letters on them. One had been made by a friend. It had a nun, gimmel, hay, and shin. These are the first letters in the saying **Nes gadol hayah sham,** "A great miracle happened there." The other

How to Light a Ḥanukkiyah

Each night of Ḥanukkah, we light an additional candle using the **shamash** (שַׁמָּשׁ), the "helper" candle. On the first night, we place one candle on the right side of the ḥanukkiyah and light it using the shamash. The second night, we place two candles on the right side and light them starting with the new candle. And so on. On the eighth night, all eight candles plus the shamash burn brightly.

Some families light one ḥanukkiyah; others light one ḥanukkiyah for each member of the family. Which night of Ḥanukkah is shown here? How do you know?

dreidel, a gift from Rivkah, had been made in Israel. Instead of a Shin, it had a Pay, which stands for the word Po, meaning "here." *"Of course,"* Daniel thought, "the story of Ḥanukkah happened in Israel. That's why Israelis say 'here.'"

Light the Ḥanukkiyah

A ḥanukkiyah can be made of clay, metal, or glass. It can be any shape or size as long as it has space for eight candles plus a shamash.

Connect the dots to see the ḥanukkiyah. Then color the ḥanukkiyah, and add the shamash and candles for the third night.

Draw a flame on each candle. Which flame will you draw first? Why?

_____

_____

_____

_____

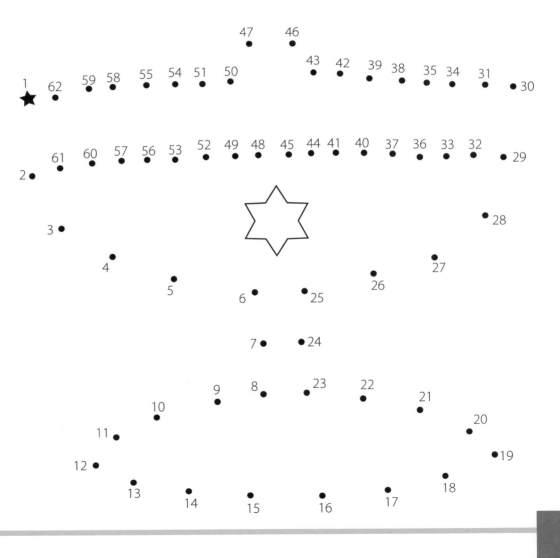

Playing Dreidel

Start with an equal number of tokens—pennies or chocolate coins called, "Ḥanukkah gelt"—for each player. Have each player put 1 token into the "pot." Give each player a turn spinning the dreidel. If it lands on

נ Nun—the player gets nothing;

ג Gimmel—the player gets everything, and the other players refill the pot by each putting in 1 token;

ה Hay—the player takes half the pot;

ש Shin—the player puts one token in the pot. (In Israel, these are the directions for the letter Pay.)

At the end, the person with the most tokens wins.

Ḥanukkah gelt that's made of chocolate is fun to play with and just as much fun to eat. Yummy!

What Do You Do?

Imagine that you are playing dreidel. What should you do when the dreidel lands on:

_____ _____ _____

_____ _____

Circle the letter that tells you that the dreidel is used in Israel.

Daniel v-mailed Rivkah and then went to ElijahRocks. Rivkah arrived a minute later and Elijah welcomed them both. "I see you remembered that Ḥanukkah starts tomorrow," he said. "Please sit and I'll tell you how the holiday came to be.

"More than 2,000 years ago, Israel was ruled by the Syrians. The Syrians followed Greek customs and traditions. They spoke Greek, dressed like Greeks, and read Greek books. Many Jews began to accept Greek ways, too. They played the games that the Greeks played when they worshipped their gods. This worried and angered some Jews. They were afraid that Jews who behaved like Greeks would stop being Jewish.

"And then Antiochus, the Syrian king, decided to force all the Jews to stop being Jewish. He said Jews could no longer study Torah. He also ordered them to stop celebrating

The official seal of the modern State of Israel includes two olive branches, symbols of peace, and a seven-branch menorah, a reminder of the ancient Temple in Jerusalem.

Shabbat and Jewish festivals and to start worshipping the Greek gods.

"On the 25th day of the Hebrew month of Kislev, the Syrians entered the Temple in Jerusalem, the holiest place of the Jewish people. The Syrians put out the flame of the Temple's Eternal Light, the **Ner Tamid.** The Eternal Light was the **Menorah,** or candlestick with seven branches, whose light had burned day and night as a sign of God's constant presence. The Syrians then placed statues of the Greek gods—idols—in the Temple.

"A brave man named Mattathias lived in Modi'in, not far from Jerusalem. He and his five sons led a revolt against the Syrians. Mattathias declared, 'Whoever is for God, follow me.' The rebels hid in the hills and other Jews joined them. Mattathias's son Judah became their leader after his father died. He became known as Judah the Maccabee, or Judah the Hammer. His fighters were called Maccabees.

"The Syrians had a huge army and many weapons. The Maccabees were a small group with few weapons. But they knew the best places to hide and then attack the Syrians. They fought hard for three long years. Finally, they drove Antiochus's army out of Jerusalem.

"When the Jews came back to the Temple, they destroyed the idols, cleaned the Temple, rebuilt the altar to God, and relit the Temple's Menorah. On the 25th day of Kislev, three years after the Syrians had entered the Temple, the Jews rededicated the Temple to God."

"The Hebrew word for 'dedication' is ḥanukkah. That is how the holiday got its name," chimed in Rivkah. "And it is also called the Festival of Lights, or **Ḥag Ha'urim**."

"Yes, it is a holiday of light and hope," said Elijah. "Our people's victory over a large and powerful enemy was a miracle. The story teaches us to be proud and strong Jews." With that, Elijah wished the cousins a happy Ḥanukkah and disappeared.

On Ḥanukkah, it is a custom to eat foods that have been fried in oil, like jelly donuts, known in Hebrew as *sufganiyot,* and potato pancakes, or latkes. The custom reminds us of the legend of the oil. What is your favorite Ḥanukkah food?

"Let's go!" Daniel said. And they quickly selected the Treasure Trail.

Ḥanukkah Riddle

In the deepest dark of winter night, what shines big and bright?

When the riddle faded, Daniel and Rivkah were standing in the courtyard of the ancient Temple in Jerusalem. Their regular clothes had been transformed into the robes of ancient Israel. The courtyard was filled with men and women dressed like them, praising God because the Syrian army had been driven out of the city. The cousins watched as Jews destroyed the Greek idols and scrubbed, patched, and polished the Temple.

Moving toward the area where the Temple's Menorah was about to be lit, they overheard a man cry out, "What shall we do? There is just enough oil to keep the light of the Menorah burning for only one day. It will take a week before fresh oil is ready."

A woman next to him spoke up. "Let us use the oil we have, start to make more, and pray for a miracle."

"That's it!" said Daniel. "This is the legend of the Ḥanukkah miracle. It tells how enough oil for only one day lasted for eight days. The answer to the riddle is the light of the Ḥanukkah menorah. It reminds us that God is always present, even in the dark of winter."

(This story is based on a legend from the Talmud, Shabbat 21b.*)*

The riddle had been solved! Rivkah and Daniel were transported to their homes, eager to celebrate the holiday.

When your teacher says it is OK, turn to the Treasure Trail on pages 10–11 and place the Ḥanukkah sticker in the correct spot.

www.ElijahRocks.net

Add to the Light of Your Ḥanukkiyah

The light of the Ḥanukkah candles reminds us of God's presence. You can add to that light by following in God's kind and caring ways. How can you do that?

_____

_____

_____

Tishre	תִּשְׁרֵי
Ḥeshvan	חֶשְׁוָן
Kislev	כִּסְלֵו
Tevet	טֵבֵת
Shevat 15	שְׁבָט
Adar	אֲדָר
Nisan	נִיסָן
Iyar	אִיָּר
Sivan	סִיוָן
Tammuz	תַּמּוּז
Av	אָב
Elul	אֱלוּל

CHAPTER 8

Tu BiShevat

Daniel shivered as he got out of bed. There was frost on the windows and the wind was howling.

"Happy Tu BiShevat," Daniel's mom greeted him. "Today is the birthday of the trees. The synagogue is having a **Tu BiShevat seder,** the holiday meal, this afternoon. Please be home by 3:30 so we can get there on time."

A Birthday for Trees?

The Torah teaches us to respect all life, including plant life and trees. It tells how God commanded our ancestors not to eat the fruit of a tree for three years after it was planted. In the fourth year, they had to give the fruit as an offering to God. Finally, they could eat the fruit once a tree became five years old (Leviticus 19:23–25).

But there are millions and millions of trees in Israel. It would be hard to remember exactly when each one was planted. So the years of a tree's life are counted from one Tu BiShevat to the next. Tu BiShevat is the new year—and the birthday—of the trees.

Name another holiday that celebrates a new year in Jewish life. *Hint:* It's a honey of a holiday.

_____

A Tu BiShevat Seder

At a Tu BiShevat seder, we thank God for the gifts of nature, especially for trees. We eat fruits that have peels or shells that need to be removed—like oranges, grapefruits, and almonds. (Nuts are a type of fruit.) We eat fruits that have a pit—like dates, peaches, and olives. (Yup, olives are a fruit, too.) And we eat fruits that have tiny seeds inside, fruits that can be eaten whole—like raisins, figs, and berries.

We drink four kinds of wine or grape juice—white, white mixed with a little red, red mixed with a little white, and red. We recite the blessings over fruit and wine, and thank God for all the good things that trees give us.

Write a birthday wish or blessing for the trees near your home or school.

_____

_____

True or False?

Write a T or an F next to each statement to show that it is either True or False.

1. Trees are homes for some animals. _____

2. Paper is made from trees. _____

3. Trees provide shade. _____

4. Trees provide food for people and animals. _____

5. Wood for furniture comes from trees. _____

6. Money grows on trees. _____

7. Fruits and nuts grow on trees. _____

8. Dogs get their bark from trees. _____

Describe your favorite kind of tree and why you like it. _____

_____

_____

שבעת
המינים

*Seven
Species*

The Bible teaches that there are seven types, or species, of fruits and grains—wheat, barley, grapes, figs, pomegranates, olives, and dates—that are special crops of Israel. On Tu BiShevat it is a tradition to eat fruit from Israel.

This is a Tu BiShevat fruit platter. The blessing over fruit is under the picture of the trees and fruit basket. What fruits would you like to serve on the platter?

This clock in Tel Aviv uses Hebrew letters instead of numbers. Which letter do you think has the value of 5? Why do you think so?

"It's strange that we celebrate Tu BiShevat in the middle of the winter," Daniel said.

"But in Israel the winter rains have mostly stopped by the end of January or in February, the weather is warmer, and green buds have begun to appear," his mom answered.

"I'd better v-mail Rivkah and go to ElijahRocks before I leave for school," Daniel thought.

Letters That Count

Each letter of the Hebrew alphabet stands for a number. For example, א (alef) = 1, ב (bet) = 2, and ג (gimmel) = 3.

ט"וּ בִּשְׁבָט (Tu BiShevat) falls on the 15th day of שְׁבָט (Shevat). ט (tet) = 9, and ו (vav) = 6. When the letters ט and ו are put together—ט"וּ—they add up to 15 and make the sound Tu. That is how the holiday got its name.

As soon as Daniel and Rivkah arrived, Elijah appeared carrying a platter of figs, dates, pomegranates, apricots, almonds, sunflower seeds, and carob-covered raisins. "My Tu BiShevat seder starts in an hour," he said.

"Everyone in my religious school donates money to plant trees in Israel," said Daniel. "You can receive a certificate for the trees you plant that honor someone special to you. It's a mitzvah to plant a tree.

"Since the 1970s, Tu BiShevat has become a holiday on which we not only celebrate the gifts of nature," Daniel continued, "but also renew our commitment to care for the environment. We make efforts to use water and energy—like gasoline and electricity—wisely, to plant trees, and to recycle paper, glass, and metal."

Trees can help athletes become strong by providing yummy fruits that are chock-full of vitamins and minerals. Who else can trees help? How?

How can recycling newspapers help care for the world? How can riding a bicycle help? What other pluses are there to riding a bicycle?

81

Tu BiShevat Riddle

What do we owe to planet Earth and to each generation to which we give birth?

"Oops! My guests and I will be planting a tree. I better get ready," said Elijah, picking up his fruit platter and waving goodbye. The cousins quickly selected the Treasure Trail.

When the riddle faded, the cousins watched as, a few feet away from them, an old woman dug a hole in the soil and planted a tiny carob tree seedling.

Rivkah walked up to the woman and said, "I hope I'm not being rude, but it takes seventy years for a carob tree to bear fruit. Do you expect to live long enough to eat the fruit of your tree?"

The old woman chuckled. "I found the world filled with carob trees because my parents and grandparents planted them for me. Now I am planting one for my children and grandchildren."

(This story is based on a legend from the Talmud, Ta'anit 23a.)

"That's the answer to the riddle," Daniel said. "We should plant trees and care for nature so that the next generation can share in the goodness that our parents passed on to us."

Kaboom! Daniel was transported home. He grabbed his backpack and rushed off to school, thinking about the sweet fruits of Israel awaiting him at the Tu BiShevat seder.

When your teacher says it is OK, turn to the Treasure Trail on pages 10–11 and place the Tu BiShevat sticker in the correct spot.

www.ElijahRocks.net

Tishre	תִּשְׁרֵי
Ḥeshvan	חֶשְׁוָן
Kislev	כִּסְלֵו
Tevet	טֵבֵת
Shevat	שְׁבָט
Adar ⑭	אֲדָר
Nisan	נִיסָן
Iyar	אִיָּר
Sivan	סִיוָן
Tammuz	תַּמּוּז
Av	אָב
Elul	אֱלוּל

CHAPTER 9

Purim

Daniel's VPI beeped. It was Rivkah. "Let's go to ElijahRocks now," she wrote. "Later on I won't have time because I'll need to help my mom prepare **mishlo'aḥ manot**—baskets of **hamantashen,** fruit, and candy. We give them to our family and friends to wish them a happy Purim."

"We order those baskets from our synagogue and send them to people we know," Daniel replied. "We call them by their Yiddish name, **shalaḥ manos.** Let's go."

A Purim Treat That's Great to Eat

On Purim, we eat hamantashen—triangle-shaped pastries filled with jam or poppy seeds or even chocolate. The name "hamantash" comes from Yiddish. It means "Haman's pocket" or "poppy-seed-filled pouch." In Hebrew, the pastries are called *oznei Haman,* meaning "Haman's ears."

What is your favorite hamantash filling?

_____

What costume would you like to wear on Purim? Why?

What would you want to include in a gift of mishlo'aḥ manot?

As always, Elijah was there to greet them. Daniel and Rivkah giggled because today he wore a purple robe with green stripes and big, floppy clown shoes. He had on a round red nose and his hair was covered by a yellow mop head and a funny hat.

"I'm glad you like my Purim costume," Elijah said. "It's fun to dress up in costumes on Purim. Some synagogues even have a Purim carnival. We also read the story of Purim, which teaches important lessons."

"Ooh! Let me tell the story!" Rivkah pleaded. Elijah nodded, and she began. "A long, long time ago in the city of Shushan, in the country of Persia, there lived a king named Ahasuerus. He had a beautiful queen, Esther. The king did not know that Esther was Jewish.

In towns and cities throughout Israel, there are Purim parades called "Ad Lo Yada." At these celebrations, people dress in costumes and there are colorful floats, music, and dance performances.

Scrolling Along

We read the Purim story in a book from the Bible called the Scroll of Esther, **Megillat Esther. Megillah** (מְגִלָּה) means "scroll." Unlike a Torah scroll, which has two wooden rollers, the Scroll of Esther has only one wooden roller.

Some Megillat Esther scrolls are illustrated. If you were illustrating a Scroll of Esther, what would you draw? Why?

"Ahasuerus had an evil chief officer, Haman. Haman made people bow down to him."

Daniel jumped in, "Esther's cousin Mordecai had once saved the king's life. But Haman didn't know that. All he knew was that Mordecai would not bow down to him because Jews bow only to God. That made Haman so angry he decided to have Mordecai and all the Jews in the Land of Persia killed.

"Haman cast lots, which is like drawing a number out of a hat, to decide the day on which the Jews would be killed. The Hebrew word for lots is *purim.* The lot fell on the 13th day of the Hebrew month of Adar. Then, Haman went to Ahasuerus to arrange for a royal order decreeing that all the Jews be killed on the 13th of Adar."

We show that we are thankful for the goodness in our lives by giving gifts of food not only to friends and family but also to those in need.

It's a Mitzvah to Make Noise

During the megillah reading, we use twirling noisemakers, called **graggers,** to drown out Haman's name when it is read aloud. Some people stamp their feet and hiss or yell "boo" when they hear Haman's name. This reminds us to use our voices to speak out louder than the voices of evil. Jewish tradition teaches us to be brave, to speak up about fairness and peace.

Decorate the gragger with a character from the Purim story.

Purim Riddle

How do we turn a wrong into a right? What must we do with all our might?

Suddenly Rivkah and Daniel looked around. Elijah had vanished. Taking the hint to move on, the cousins immediately selected the TreasureTrail.

When the riddle faded, the cousins were standing behind a column in the royal court where Ahasuerus sat on his throne. Esther entered the room. Rivkah and Daniel knew that it was forbidden to go uninvited before the king. Esther had not been invited. She was willing to risk her life to save her people.

As soon as Ahasuerus saw Esther, his eyes lit up. He held out his golden scepter, or rod, to welcome her. Pleased, Esther invited the king and Haman to two feasts. At the second feast, when the king asked her what wish he could grant her, Esther spoke out. "I am a Jew. Wicked Haman has plotted to kill me and all my people. Please save us!"

Ahasuerus quickly took action. Haman was hanged in place of Mordecai, and Mordecai replaced Haman as the king's chief officer.

As Esther passed through the archway she spied Rivkah and Daniel. "There shall be light and celebration for all the Jews on the 14th day of Adar," she said. *(The story is based on the Scroll of Esther.)*

"Wow! It took courage to speak out against Haman's evil plan," Daniel said. "That's the answer to the riddle. Speaking out with all your might is how we turn a wrong into a right."

"I'll v-mail you a basket of mishlo'aḥ manot," Rivkah quickly called out. Then, before they could wave goodbye, they were transported home.

➡ *When your teacher says it is OK, turn to the Treasure Trail on pages 10–11 and place the Purim sticker in the correct spot.*

www.ElijahRocks.net

Tishre	תִּשְׁרֵי
Ḥeshvan	חֶשְׁוָן
Kislev	כִּסְלֵו
Tevet	טֵבֵת
Shevat	שְׁבָט
Adar	אֲדָר
Nisan	15	נִיסָן
Iyar	אִיָּר
Sivan	סִיוָן
Tammuz	תַּמּוּז
Av	אָב
Elul	אֱלוּל

CHAPTER 10

פֶּסַח

Passover

Spring had arrived. The weather was warmer and the tulips were in bloom. Daniel's family would be hosting the **Passover seder,** the holiday meal celebrating the Exodus, our freedom from slavery in Egypt. Eighteen guests were coming—aunts, uncles, cousins, and friends.

Tonight the family was cleaning out the **ḥametz** from their home. Ḥametz is food that is made with an ingredient that causes the food to rise. For example, bread and many cakes and cookies are made with yeast, which causes dough to rise. So they are ḥametz.

Traditionally, ḥametz is not eaten or even kept in the house on Passover, **Pesaḥ**. Instead, we eat **matzah** (מַצָּה) and other holiday foods that are kosher for Passover.

Daniel's father placed the Passover candlesticks on the table. Then came one wine glass and one **haggadah** (הַגָּדָה)—the

We recite the blessing over wine and drink the wine four times at the seder. Each cup reminds us of a promise God made in the Torah: "I will free you from Egypt." "I will deliver you from slavery." "I will lead you home." "You will be my people."

Why Matzah?

Jewish tradition teaches that when our people were freed from slavery, they left Egypt so quickly that they had no time to let their dough rise. They put the dough on their backs and the sun baked it into hard, flat loaves. On Passover, we eat matzah to remind ourselves of our ancestors' hardship.

At the seder, the leader raises the matzah and says, "This is the bread of hardship. . . . Let everyone who is hungry come and eat." The matzah reminds us not only to invite guests to our seder, but also to help people in need.

Afikoman

We put a plate with three sheets of matzah on the seder table. During the seder, we break off a piece from the middle matzah and hide it. It is called the **afikoman**. In some families, the adults hide the afikoman, and the children find it. In other families, the children hide it, and the adults find it. A prize is given either to the person who finds the afikoman or to the one who hides it so well that it cannot be found. Everyone eats a piece of the afikoman at dessert time.

Where is the best place to hide the afikoman in your home? Why?

_____

_____

Matzah is flat because there is no yeast in it.

book with the story of Passover and the holiday blessings and songs—for each person at the seder. "Tomorrow we will read from the haggadah," said Daniel's dad.

"We tell the story of Passover as if God had freed each of us personally from slavery in Egypt. Daniel, the **Four Questions,** which you will ask, remind us that we are now free people. Only free people can ask questions."

95

This Israeli family, originally from Yemen, has many guests at its seder. Do you prefer to be a guest or a host at a seder? Why?

"I'll go practice," Daniel said. Later that day Daniel went to ElijahRocks. Rivkah was already there.

"Let's review the story of Passover," Elijah said. "I'll begin and you can jump in whenever you want.

"More than 3,000 years ago, our people lived in the Land of Egypt. We were called **Israelites** and were ruled by a king called the **Pharaoh.** The Torah tells us that Pharaoh made us slaves. He forced us to work hard making bricks of clay. The cruel masters he put in charge of us beat us. Still, Pharaoh feared that we would grow in numbers and join his enemies. So he ordered his servants to drown our baby boys in the Nile River."

"But one boy was saved," said Rivkah. "His mother put him in a basket and set it among the reeds of the Nile River. His sister watched over him from a distance. Pharaoh's daughter found the baby and took pity on him. She named him **Moses** and raised him as her son."

"Excellent," said Elijah. "When Moses grew up, he left Egypt. One day, he saw a bush burning in the desert, but the flames did not destroy it! Suddenly, he heard God's voice coming out of the burning bush. Moses heard God command him to help free the Israelites from slavery."

"Moses obeyed God and went to Pharaoh saying, 'Let my people go!'" continued Daniel. "But Pharaoh was stubborn, and he said no.

"Because of his stubbornness, God sent ten terrible punishments—the **Ten Plagues**. After each of the first nine plagues, Moses asked Pharaoh to free the Israelites. But Pharaoh had a hard heart, and he refused. So God sent another plague. Finally, the tenth plague—the most terrible of all—came. It was the plague of death.

The Ten Plagues

1. The Nile River turned to blood (דָּם).
2. Frogs covered the land (צְפַרְדֵּעַ).
3. The dust of the earth turned into wingless bugs (כִּנִּים).
4. God sent millions of insects (עָרוֹב).
5. All the cattle died (דֶּבֶר).
6. The Egyptians were covered with sores (שְׁחִין).
7. Sharp, icy hailstones fell from the sky (בָּרָד).
8. Millions of insects called locusts ate the crops (אַרְבֶּה).
9. A heavy darkness covered Egypt (חֹשֶׁךְ).
10. The Egyptians' firstborn sons were killed (מַכַּת בְּכוֹרוֹת).

The Seder Plate

At the center of the seder table is the seder plate. These are the foods we put on it.

1. **Karpas** (כַּרְפַּס): a potato or green herb, like parsley, to remind us of spring. We dip the parsley in salt water to remember the tears our people cried in Egypt.

2. **Roasted Egg** (בֵּיצָה): a reminder of the festival sacrifice in the Temple in Jerusalem.

3. **Maror** (מָרוֹר): a bitter herb, like horseradish, to remind us of the bitterness of slavery.

4. **Zeroa** (זְרוֹעַ): a roasted bone (vegetarians use a red beet) to remind us of the Passover sacrifice that was offered in the Temple in Jerusalem.

5. **Ḥaroset** (חֲרוֹסֶת): a mixture of fruit, wine, and nuts to remind us of the bricks that Pharaoh forced the Israelites to make.

6. **Ḥazeret** (חֲזֶרֶת): an additional bitter herb, like romaine lettuce, that some people place on their seder plate.

Which food on the seder plate do you like most? Why?

_____

Which do you like least? Why?

_____

What food might you want to add to the seder plate? Why?

_____

"Every firstborn child in Egypt died, even Pharaoh's son. But the Israelite children lived. The plague passed over their homes. That is why the holiday is called Passover."

"The last plague broke Pharaoh's hard heart," said Rivkah. "'Go!' he cried. 'Take your people from this land.' So Moses led the Israelites out of Egypt."

Sense Something Special?

We use all our senses at the Passover seder. On the lines next to the drawing, write two things at the seder that you can:

SEE   HEAR   TOUCH   TASTE   SMELL

You can choose some of your items from this list.

Maror   Grape juice   Haroset
Haggadah   Matzah   Four Questions

"You're both really good. You don't need my help to tell the story," said Elijah. "So I'll be off to tidy up my chariot and get ready to go from seder to seder. Ḥag samayaḥ!"

"Let's head for the Treasure Trail," said Rivkah.

Passover Riddle

What must we do now that we're free? It's why God helped us cross the sea.

When the riddle faded, Daniel and Rivkah were dressed in long robes, like Elijah. Surrounding them were thousands of newly freed Israelite slaves. In the distance, there was a loud noise—Pharaoh and his army! Pharaoh had changed his mind and was coming after the Israelites. There was no way to escape. The army chased the Israelites to the edge of the Sea of Reeds.

Moses raised his arm over the sea and a great wind came from God. It pushed apart the waters, creating a path of dry land. Daniel and Rivkah joined the Israelites as they quickly crossed to the other side. When the Egyptian army followed them into the sea, the waters came together, drowning Pharaoh and his soldiers.

"Now we are free to worship God," the Israelites cried out. *(The story is based on the Book of Exodus 14:8–30.)*

"One way to worship God is to help others who are not yet free or who are hungry," Daniel said. "It's an important reason why we were given freedom." That was the answer to the riddle. In a flash, they were home—free, happy, and ready for Passover!

Elijah's and Miriam's Cups

We fill a special cup, the **Cup of Elijah,** with wine at our seder. Toward the end of the seder, we stand and open the door as if we were welcoming Elijah into our home. Jewish tradition teaches that Elijah will bring the time of peace. Each year, we hope that our wish for peace will come true soon.

Some families also put the **Cup of Miriam** on their seder table. Miriam's cup is filled with spring water. It reminds us of the ancient teaching that Miriam's well followed the Israelites through the desert. Just as Miriam's watching over Moses had helped keep him safe and alive, the well gave the Israelites the water that helped keep *them* alive.

Elijah's and Miriam's Cups

At the seder we drink wine to celebrate the gift of freedom. But sadly, others lost their lives as we gained our freedom. So we remove ten drops of wine from our cup of joy when we say the names of the plagues. What does that teach us about the value of all human life?

When your teacher says it is OK, turn to the Treasure Trail on pages 10–11 and place the Passover sticker in the correct spot.

www.ElijahRocks.net

Hmm. I wonder whether Miriam knows that both of us are honored at the seder table.

103

Tishre		תִּשְׁרֵי
Ḥeshvan		חֶשְׁוָן
Kislev		כִּסְלֵו
Tevet		טֵבֵת
Shevat		שְׁבָט
Adar		אֲדָר
Nisan	27	נִיסָן
Iyar		אִיָּר
Sivan		סִיוָן
Tammuz		תַּמּוּז
Av		אָב
Elul		אֱלוּל

CHAPTER 11

יוֹם הַשּׁוֹאָה

Yom Hashoah

Most Jewish holidays are happy times. But some Jewish holidays help us remember sad times so that they can teach us important lessons about how to live better lives.

Around the time when your great-grandparents were born, a great tragedy happened to our people. An evil man named Adolf Hitler ruled Germany. Hitler wanted to kill all the Jews.

Some Jews escaped to other countries; some went into hiding; and some were able to fight back. But many, many Jewish men, women, and children in Europe were murdered by Hitler and his followers. Other innocent people were also murdered. This happened during World War II.

Every year, we set aside a day to remember the millions who died in what we call the Holocaust. That day is called **Holocaust Memorial Day,** or in Hebrew, **Yom Hashoah**. But the full name is **Holocaust Martyrs' and Heroes' Remembrance Day** because we also remember that many brave Jews and non-Jews fought back and saved lives.

On this holy day, there are prayer services in synagogues. We light a memorial candle—which is often yellow—in memory of the Jews who were killed. We also recite the mourner's prayer, the **Kaddish,** for them.

We must never forget that people can choose to be cruel or kind. Remembering can help us prevent such a terrible thing from happening again.

 When your teacher says it is OK, turn to the Treasure Trail on pages 10–11 and place the Yom Hashoah sticker in the correct spot.

What can you do if you see a bully being mean to someone?

Tishre	תִּשְׁרֵי
Ḥeshvan	חֶשְׁוָן
Kislev	כִּסְלֵו
Tevet	טֵבֵת
Shevat	שְׁבָט
Adar	אֲדָר
Nisan	נִיסָן
Iyar 5	אִיָּר
Sivan	סִיוָן
Tammuz	תַּמּוּז
Av	אָב
Elul	אֱלוּל

יוֹם הָעַצְמָאוּת

Yom Ha'atzma'ut

The week after Passover, Rivkah v-mailed Daniel. "Israel's Independence Day—Yom Ha'atzma'ut—is almost here," she wrote. "It's like the Fourth of July in the United States.

"On Yom Ha'atzma'ut, we celebrate the creation of the modern State of Israel in 1948. It comes on the fifth day of the Hebrew month of Iyar, which is usually in May. Like other Jewish holidays, such as Rosh Hashanah and Passover, it is a national holiday. So we have off from school!

The Ancient Jewish Homeland

Long ago, in the time of the Bible, the Jews lived in one land—**Eretz Yisrael** (אֶרֶץ יִשְׂרָאֵל). Abraham and Sarah were the first Jews to live in Eretz Yisrael. Their family grew and became the nation of Israel. Mighty kings, like David and Solomon, ruled. The Holy Temple was built in Jerusalem, the capital of the Jewish nation.

Then, about 2,000 years ago, foreigners conquered the land and destroyed the Temple. While some Jews remained in Eretz Yisrael, many moved to faraway places around the world. More and more Jews began to live outside Eretz Yisrael. But we never forgot our homeland. It was always in our prayers. We faced Jerusalem when we prayed, longing to return to the home of our people.

Since ancient times, camels have roamed the Land of Israel. When you visit our homeland, you can take a camel ride.

"We learned about the creation of the modern State of Israel in religious school," Daniel wrote back. "For centuries, many Jews lived in countries where they were not welcome. A man named **Theodor Herzl** believed that, as in ancient times, there should be a Jewish country, a place where Jews could live in freedom and peace. The belief that Eretz Yisrael should be a Jewish country is

Rebuilding the Land

About 120 years ago, a group of Russian Jews moved to Eretz Yisrael, which was then called **Palestine.** There they found many Arab villages. Much of the land the newcomers wanted to farm was filled with muddy swamps or dry, hot deserts. Also, there were many diseases, like malaria, and there was not much food or water.

The newcomers planted trees, drained the swamps, and learned to farm. More and more Jews moved to Palestine. Some built large farms, called *kibbutzim*, where they lived and worked together. Others settled in cities like Jerusalem and Haifa, and lived alongside the Arabs. Yet others built new cities, like Tel Aviv. They built roads, houses, schools, libraries, and hospitals.

You're the Artist!

Imagine that you were living in Jerusalem 120 years ago. Draw a picture showing your life there. Write a caption for the picture telling how it felt to help rebuild the Jewish homeland.

Going Up

The Hebrew word **aliyah** means "rise" or "go up." Moving to Israel is called making aliyah. The honor of being called to the Torah during synagogue services is called an aliyah.

Why do you think our tradition teaches that both to settle in Israel and to be called to the Torah are to go up?

_____

_____

known as **Zionism.** Theodor Herzl is called the Father of Zionism.

"After the Holocaust, many of the Jews who had survived wanted to leave Europe. They wanted to help build the Jewish homeland. But Palestine did not belong to the Jews. So it was hard to get permission to move there. Finally, in 1947, the United Nations voted to create a Jewish state in the Land of Israel.

"On May 14, 1948, the Jews in Eretz Yisrael declared independence. They named their country the State of Israel, **Medinat Yisrael.** Jews around the world celebrated by dancing in the streets and singing **'Hatikvah,'** which later became Israel's national anthem.

"But the Arabs in Palestine and the surrounding countries did not want a Jewish state in Palestine. So on May 15, Israel was attacked by nearby Arab countries. With only a small army and a few airplanes, the Jews defended their new country. They won the war.

"For the first time in almost 2,000 years, there was a Jewish state, a place where every Jew was welcome. Jews moved to Israel from many countries. Some came from places where they had been mistreated, like North Africa and Europe. In Israel, they were free to live as Jews."

"Wow, you know a lot," said Rivkah. "Now let's VPI ourselves to ElijahRocks."

When they arrived, they were greeted by Elijah. He asked about their holiday plans.

"I haven't decided yet," said Rivkah. "In Israel, we have parades, fireworks, carnivals, street fairs, barbecues, and block parties where people sing

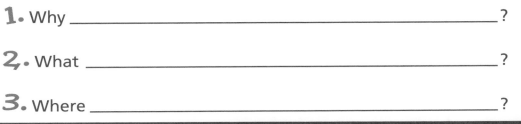

Why? What? Where?

Imagine that you have a friend who lives in Israel. List three questions you would want to ask that friend about Israel.

1. Why _____?

2. What _____?

3. Where _____?

One way to show your love of our homeland is by learning about it. The State of Israel is about the size of New Jersey. Jerusalem is in central Israel. Haifa is in the north and the Negev Desert is in the south. What else do you know about Israel?

Israel is the homeland of the Jewish people. People of many other religions, such as Muslims and Christians, also live there. This photograph shows the golden Dome of the Rock, a Muslim holy place in Jerusalem. The Western Wall, a remnant of our Holy Temple, is on the right.

The Israeli Flag

The Israeli flag is white with blue stripes, like the stripes on a prayer shawl, a tallit. It has a blue Star of David, or Magen David, in the center.

Underline the star below that appears on the U.S. flag. Circle the Star of David.

Old Glory is a name for the U.S. flag. What name might you give to the Israeli flag? Why?

_____

_____

Color the stripes and star on this Israeli flag bright blue.

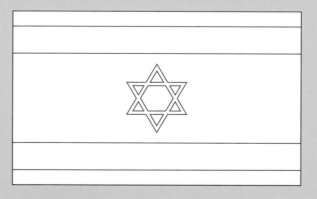

Israeli oldies. We also recite prayers for peace and thank God for the Jewish state."

"I'll go to the Yom Ha'atzma'ut fair at our synagogue," said Daniel. "We'll have a party in religious school. We'll eat Israeli foods, like ḥummus and falafel, and sing Israeli songs, including 'Hatikvah.' On Sunday, I'll march with my synagogue in the Salute to Israel Parade."

Say It in Hebrew

In Israel, Hebrew is the language of prayer *and* daily life. About 125 years ago, a man named Eliezer Ben-Yehuda created new Hebrew words to describe things that didn't exist in the time of the Bible, such as telephones, trains, and clocks.

Ben-Yehuda often used older Hebrew words to create new words. For example, *rakevet* (רַכֶּבֶת), meaning "train," is built on the root, or main letters, of the ancient Hebrew word for chariot. Try to find the Hebrew word for train in this poster.

Falafel sandwiches are traditionally made with pita bread, salad, and tahini sauce. Falafel is made from chickpeas. Tahini sauce is made from sesame seeds.

Yom Ha'atzma'ut Riddle

What says "up" and invites us to rise? It's something we value, something we prize.

"It sounds like fun. Even though you won't see me, I'll be looking for you on Sunday," Elijah said as he vanished. The cousins quickly selected the Treasure Trail.

When the riddle faded, Daniel and Rivkah were standing in Shuk Hacarmel, Tel Aviv's open-air market. There were hundreds of stalls, selling everything—pots and pans, T-shirts, video games. Best of all was the food.

Around them, the crowds shopped for their holiday picnics. People spoke many different languages, including Hebrew, French, Russian, English, Arabic, and Yiddish.

"I've got the answer to the riddle!" said Rivkah. "Shuk Hacarmel is filled with Jews from around the world. To move to Israel is to make aliyah, meaning 'to go up.'"

It was the right answer to the riddle. So in an instant, Rivkah and Daniel were transported home. They lost no time getting ready for their holiday celebrations.

When your teacher says it is OK, turn to the Treasure Trail on pages 10–11 and place the Yom Ha'atzma'ut sticker in the correct spot.

www.ElijahRocks.net

Tishre	תִּשְׁרֵי
Ḥeshvan	חֶשְׁוָן
Kislev	כִּסְלֵו
Tevet	טֵבֵת
Shevat	שְׁבָט
Adar	אֲדָר
Nisan	נִיסָן
Iyar	אִיָּר
Sivan 6	סִיוָן
Tammuz	תַּמּוּז
Av	אָב
Elul	אֱלוּל

CHAPTER 13

שָׁבוּעוֹת

Shavuot

Daniel was excited. In a few weeks, he would be on summer vacation and would visit Rivkah in Eilat. Eilat is a city in southern Israel, near the Sinai Desert.

The Bible teaches that the Israelites wandered through the Sinai after they were freed from slavery in Egypt. It also teaches that Moses went up Mount Sinai to learn the Torah from God. Daniel's rabbi said, "The Torah is God's gift to us. It teaches us how to live as a free and strong people. We are strong when we follow the instructions of the Torah by

The Torah teaches that it is our responsibility to do what is good and right. Why might treating your family with kindness and love not only be good and right but also add to your happiness?

performing mitzvot, like reciting blessings or visiting people who are ill. Shavuot is sometimes called **Zeman Matan Torataynu,** Time of the Giving of Our Torah."

Mrs. Lubar said, "Shavuot celebrates the giving of the Torah and the early-summer harvest. After crossing the Sinai Desert, the Israelites entered the Land of Israel and became farmers. They knew that seven weeks after the beginning of Passover, their wheat and fruits would be ready to harvest. They counted the forty-nine days starting from the second day of

This Torah scroll and its case were made in Iraq almost 100 years ago. Although the case may make the scroll *look* different from the Torah in your synagogue, the words are exactly the same. All Torah scrolls have the same words. But people's understandings of those words may be different.

Passover and ending on Shavout. This custom is called **counting the omer.**

"Like Sukkot and Passover, Shavuot is a pilgrimage holiday. The Israelite farmers went to the Temple in Jerusalem. They brought loaves of bread made with their new wheat, and they brought baskets of the first fruits of their harvest—figs, dates, grapes, and honey—as offerings to God. That is why Shavuot is also called **Ḥag Hakatzir,** Festival of the Grain Harvest, and **Ḥag Habikkurim,** Festival of the First Fruits."

This is an omer counter.

Counting the Days and Weeks

The Hebrew word **shavuot** means "weeks." It reminds us that there are seven weeks between Passover and Shavuot. Describe a time when you were looking forward to something so much that you counted the minutes, days, or weeks.

_____

_____

How does counting the days to a special event add to its excitement?

_____

How might counting the omer add to your celebration of Shavuot?

_____

Like our ancestors, there are Israelis who farm the land today. Their harvest is sold in supermarkets and open-air markets, like Machaneh Yehudah in Jerusalem.

Daniel's VPI beeped. Rivkah was ready to log on to ElijahRocks. They both logged on and Elijah greeted them, asking how they celebrate Shavuot.

"We go to holiday services in synagogue and decorate our home with flowers," answered Rivkah. "In some Israeli towns, there are parades on Shavuot. Children carry baskets of fruit as a reminder of the first fruits of summer that were brought to the ancient Temple. My friends and I will be in a parade."

"At home we light holiday candles, make Kiddush, recite the blessing over ḥallah, and eat dairy foods," answered Daniel.

"At synagogue services, we thank God for all the good in our lives. We read the Ten Commandments from the Torah, and we also read the Book of Ruth. Teenagers in our congregation celebrate all that they have learned about Jewish tradition and values with a Confirmation ceremony. Some grown-ups stay up late—or even all night—to study Torah."

Favorite Fruits

Draw your favorite fruits in the basket below.

On Shavuot, we especially enjoy sweet dairy foods, such as cheesecake and cheese blintzes. They remind us that the Bible describes Eretz Yisrael as "a land flowing with milk and honey."

Shavuot Riddle

What must our people honor and do to treasure God's gift and forever be true?

"Sounds like you're ready for an adventure," said Elijah. "So Ḥag Samayaḥ! I'm off to make my cheesecake and blintzes." Elijah vanished, and the cousins selected the Treasure Trail.

When the riddle had faded away, Rivkah and Daniel were standing at the foot of a great mountain. It was Mount Sinai! Like the hundreds of thousands of Israelites around them, the cousins were dressed in long robes.

The crash of thunder filled their ears. They looked up and saw a pitch-black sky streaked by bolts of lightning. The blast of a shofar grew louder and louder. Then, suddenly, all was silent.

Daniel and Rivkah could almost hear their own hearts beat. Then, along with all our people, they received the **Ten Commandments.**

(This story is based on the Book of Exodus, chapters 19 and 20.)

Daniel could hardly speak. He whispered to Rivkah, "The Bible says that after our people received the Ten

The Ten Commandments

1. I am Adonai your God who brought you out of Egypt.

2. Do not have other gods besides Me or pray to idols.

3. Do not use My name except for holy purposes.

4. Remember Shabbat and keep it holy.

5. Honor your father and mother.

6. Do not murder.

7. Do not take another person's husband or wife.

8. Do not steal.

9. Do not tell lies about other people.

10. Do not desire what belongs to your neighbor.

Commandments, Moses learned the other mitzvot from God. Then Moses taught them to the Israelites. The answer to the riddle is that the Jewish people must honor the Torah and God by doing mitzvot, like observing the Jewish holidays and helping others."

Daniel and Rivkah were transported home for the last time. They had completed the Treasure Trail and their year of testing the VPI. They were happy to be home but sad that their adventure was over. Yet it was comforting to know that the cycle of the Jewish holidays repeats itself each year. Besides Rivkah's dad was sure to invent something new for them to test.

When your teacher says it is OK, turn to the Treasure Trail on pages 10–11 and place the Shavuot sticker in the correct spot.

www.ElijahRocks.net

Jewish Holidays
Certificate of Achievement

On this day of _____ , let it be known throughout the land
Date

that _____ has successfully completed
Name

The Jewish Holiday Treasure Trail. May _____
Name

live a life filled with love of Jewish tradition and values and

celebrate the cycle of Jewish holidays every year with family,

friends, and community.

_____
Name of School

_____
Official Signature

Credits

The publisher gratefully acknowledges the cooperation of the following sources of photographs:

David Behrman 29 (bottom); **Creative Image Photography** 28, 29 (top), 44, 57; **P. Deliss/Godong/Corbis** 84; **Fotolia** 19; **Gila Gevirtz** 38, 40, 48, 80 (bottom), 81 (bottom), 108, 110, 118, 122; **Sam and Lisa Grossman** 120 (top); **The Jewish Museum/Art Resources, NY** 120 (bottom); **Terry Kaye** 79, 115 (top); **Erich Lessing/Art Resources, NY** 80 (top); **Richard Lobell** 5, 12, 17, 18, 30, 39, 52, 54, 55, 56, 58, 64, 66, 68, 72, 86, 89, 92, 94, 95, 98, 102, 103, 115 (bottom), 121, 123; **Richard T. Nowitz/Corbis** 87, 96, 104;

Jeremy Poisson 16, 24, 26, 49; **Steve Raymer/Corbis** 37; **Réunion des Musées Nationaux/Art Resources, NY** 88; **Stockxpert** 47, 76, 114; **Ginny Twersky** 46. Cover: **Richard Lobell** with **Ginny Twersky** (scribe and boy in circle).

Special thanks to **Peachy Levy** for permitting us to include the photograph of her Torah mantel on page 47.

George Ulrich, illustrator: cover, ElijahRocks logo, stickers, and pages 2, 3, 7, 8, 10–11, 21, 27, 30, 33, 43, 51, 57, 60, 62, 74, 83, 91, 99, 101, 107, 117, 125, 128.